In The Donald's Time

In The Donald's Time

A Chapbook of Politically Progressive Poetry

by Jonel Abellanosa

©2019 Jonel Abellanosa

book design and layout: SpiNDec, Port Saint Lucie, FL
cover image: *Balancing Act*, ©2018 Kris Haggblom

All rights reserved.

No part of this book may be used or reproduced in any manner whatsoever without written permission except in the case of brief quotations embodied in critical articles and reviews. Members of educational institutions and organizations wishing to photocopy any of the work for classroom use, or authors, artists and publishers who would like to obtain permission for any material in the work, should contact the publisher.

Printed in the United States of America.

Published by Poetic Justice Books
Port Saint Lucie, Florida
www.poeticjusticebooks.com

ISBN: 978-1-950433-063

FIRST EDITION
10 9 8 7 6 5 4 3 2 1

In The Donald's Time
A Chapbook of Politically Progressive Poetry

by Jonel Abellanosa

Table of Contents

3	Convergence
4	American Cinquain
5	The Temptation of Pope Francis
6	Mindanao
9	Fish Vendor
11	Demolition Job
12	Children of the War
14	Before and After the Dictator
15	Warning: Graphic Images, Not Suitable for Children
16	Quatrains
18	Lovers in a Mural
19	Independence Day Celebrations
20	Jack
22	Aliens vs. Predators
23	Pied Piper
24	Momus
25	Penguin
26	Supermoon in the Time of Donald Trump
27	Covfefe
28	Not Just Listen, but Hear
30	The Ravaging
31	The Watchers
32	The Drought
33	Whale
35	about the author
37	acknowledgements

In The Donald's Time

Convergence

As if no one notices yet. Falling in places, with
Brexit like a planet aligning as the latest. As if
Coincidence is still the most observable. No
Doors for fleers from carnage, no asylums for
Escapers. They'd rather say no and risk Europe's
Fragmentation than be part of the solution, the
Greatest refugee crisis as if orbiting, our only
Home heating up like the fever of nationalism.
In my country Human Rights will be hanged, extra-
judicial exclusivity for the poor and powerless. We
Keep divining stars as mankind, rising among us
Leaders with iron hands, lifted to power as
Messiahs, Impunity summarily executing, murder
Negating the promised change, whim from
One man the only law. In the land of the free, where
Power is Jupiter, the worst of human nature
Quickly gains followers. In the home of the brave,
Return to a Dark Age cheers a Demagogue. It will
Shock me if, with this planetary pattern, the
Truest Racist won't be enthroned in November.
Understand – not underestimate – The Cosmic
Verity, Which (or Who) guarantees The Karmic
Whirligig. Mars should perhaps be walled for
Xenophobes, nostalgia for strongman rule
Yoked to willingness, history with the same
Zeal as the Universe granting careful wishes

American Cinquain

Never,
Perhaps in its
Entire History, has
The house been so glaringly white
Until

After
Donald strutted
In and wagged his naked
Butt, his crowd clapping, laughing and
Cheering

The Temptation of Pope Francis

Matthew 4:1 – 11 (New International Version)

Donald Trump goes to the Vatican
To challenge Pope Francis
To turn stones to bread.

He brings Pope Francis
To the highest point of the temple
And challenges the pontiff
To throw himself down.

Finally, Trump shows the pope,
From a very high mountain,
All the kingdoms of the world
And their splendor.
"All this I will give you," says Trump,
But before the billionaire dealer
Could finish what he's saying,
Pope Francis bursts into laughter.

Mindanao

What right have I, stranger to your shores,
To imagine tureens of togetherness
Holding unshattered shapes, your tables
Hosting more than familial bond?
I still read about strife in the papers
Making me see ambiguity of son from church
Arming against brother from mosque,
Wives whose smiles postpone retribution's
Ear-splitting dawn, daughters' contempt
Veils don't conceal. My mind has conjured
Inaccurate pictures, bombarded by the world's
Protracting conflicts, quests for unshaken
Homelands tainting the TV red, mythical,
Ruins from whose framed persistence germs
Of self-sustaining ideas bud and curlicue into
Substructures of belief. Phrases have to be
Retired like weary war horses: "Peace negotiations,"
"Travel advisory," possibly the country's
"Food basket," "intra-cultural tapestry."

What I remember seems clearer: living once
In Davao's infamous Agdao district
Nicknamed "Nicaragdao," after the Nicaragua
Of the Sandinista National Liberation Front's
Revolution and the Contra proxy wars
Capturing our generation's Hollywood-induced
Imagination. Peace reigned like a strongman,
Bodies of murderers, drug peddlers, petty thieves,
Swindlers and conmen dumped in swamps

The stuff of lively rumors wetting tongues for
Early morning rice cakes, hot cocoa and mangoes
In the marketplace. They joked: bones
Of criminals make the City's bedrock for more
Edifices to rise, Davao's soil being soft, they
Said, discouraging builders of empire.
They assured: no place on these 7107
Of Luzviminda's islands safer after
Midnight, barbecue joints with karaoke
And smoking blue marlin jaws fogging heaven's
Twinkling tenants with sweet invitations
To descend, the moon keeping a dilated
Vigilante eye on parks where lovers freely roamed.
If gunshot paused intimacy or revelry,
It's always only within earshot:
We who pinned the law to our hearts
Should just dismiss the flaw straightaway.

Durian's lustful smell made volcanic love
With the consenting air, breaking and electrifying
Through spine and sinew without a bomb's discourtesy.
We ate and ate till our bodies heated as if
The growing flame hungered for oxygen,
The boulevard pulling all ropes, untying knots
Of restraint, freeing flints of feeling reserved
For the long night. More than twenty years later
I still wonder if the iconic, valued monkey-eating eagle –
Which to me stands for lost remnants of your people –
Has found an unclaimed habitat

Where it can multiply reflections on
Its feathers' brown and yellow shades
Against thickening greens under its
Flights: ended threats of extinction.

Fish Vendor

News of two ships colliding –
One sinking, the other spilling oil –
Dropped like a net from the ceiling,
Catching me in my most vulnerable moment
When I don't think of tomorrows.
A tide rose in me, and I knew
It has begun again.

Rumors are as cruel,
Tales of man-eating fishes more ravenous
Than this baby clinging to my breast,
Stories of bloated bodies
Calling creatures of the depths to feast,
Desire unsated till bones lay bare,
Gorged guts redding the blues,
Driving townsfolk from our stalls.

The sea is hungriest:
When it wakes famished
It also devours our daily rations,
Money for tuition and rent.
My husband loses the will
To go on as fisherman, staying
Home where he's prone to fill
My womb's pond with his larvae,
Breeding more mouths to feed,
Recycling our poverty moons.
Reverie buoys the mind:
I picture truckloads of rice, potatoes,

Canned sardines and noodles,
Strangers handing out cash, but
Politics in our land is another
Bottomless ocean. The only help comes
From the hugest loan shark – Hope.

Demolition Job

Unless ruins put food on the table,
No one picks up the stone hammer.
Money buys brute force power protects
With truncheons. Belligerence squats on.

The rickety waits like a house of cards.
Found tarps, plasterboards, corrugated
Discards boxing paucity, hand-to-mouth
Existence on edge of collapse.

We share walls, living like canned sardines.
The day comes when money and power
Harness the workforce with constructive tools
Tearing down our ramshackle sense of security.

Helmets, shields hedging with clarity.
We back off with one foot. The land is ours
To defend. Stones of defiance fly, inciting
More of the homeless to escalate into

Confrontations. We refuse to believe
Hunger strengthens swings bringing down
Walls. On another day, demolishers they
Hire are still our brothers in poverty.

Children of the War

Forced to memorize
The bullet's alphabet, study
Arguments of machine guns,
Grenades, mortars. We'll
Have our day, or pay.

Streets couldn't keep secrets.
Death machines in the sky
Bombarding our holes.
When we found weapons without
Their warriors, we convened like men.

Favored with the will to leave,
Saddled with sacks of uncertainty,
Others swarm like ants past borders
To whatever morsels surprise hopes.
They might return one day.

Fate doesn't choose the fallen:
Some look peacefully asleep,
Woundless, without bruises,
No hints of fear in their faces
But they're dead.

We who live among ruins
Learn to survive unparented,
Conflicts claiming adults faster,
Grownups succumbing
To freedom's lies easier.

In our games we pretend
To be soldiers. In lulls some
Stoke comfort round found
Fires, too afraid to fall asleep,
Too young to be storytellers.

Before and After the Dictator

dew clings to the leaf
as long as it can
drops like the sky's answer
to the prayer of the land

blood clings to the leaf
as long as it can
drops like the sky's tear
for the people of the land

Warning: Graphic Images, Not Suitable for Children

> "*Marius the reticulated giraffe died at the Copenhagen Zoo on Sunday...The cause of death was a shotgun blast, and after a public autopsy, the animal, who was 11 feet 6 inches, was fed to the zoo's lions and other big cats.*"
> - Anger Erupts After Danish Zoo Kills a 'Surplus' Giraffe by Nelson D. Schwartz, The New York Times, February 9, 2014

        Nazi
        Eugenicists
        would
        also
        never
        pause
     to take
    into
   account
why a healthy
peaceful   lovable
giraffe   named
Marius   shouldn't
be euthanized then
dismembered so children
visiting   the zoo
may watch and see
how   civilized
hungry   lions
could   also be

Quatrains

War zone: no asylums for poets
Nor tents for refugee noons.
They'd drink sand if land were home,
Following the shadow west.

Multitudes between regime and rebellion,
Sand-etched songs holding them captives
To imagined freedom, kindling
Of speech under league of stars.

Children perfect war games: wooden
Kalashnikovs, ghost town hide
And seek. Who are their heroes?
By chance they join the really dead,

Leaving dread: skin lacerations,
Bruises, burns from bestial reprisal.
Deadly gas: they aren't asleep.
Specter of horizon's flotilla,

Ghost squadrons scattering
The dictator's henchmen –
Figments of their hopes.
Fealty is tribal demand.

If they've to kneel to a stranger
It will be on strange lands.
They've to seek out living
And kiss the ground.

Their women weigh the coldest
Silence, heavier than a mother's heart.
Tears soak the strongman's bed,
His fear inching like the day

Fate finds him and smiles.

Lovers in a Mural

We sit on the pavement earthen with spots of brown,
Above us copper red faces, everlasting.

Why are we under this full moon stained with neon?
Here, hundreds of red-stained faces, everlasting.

Your gaze shaded with resignation's deep chestnut,
Chants sounding drab, angry faces everlasting.

If only I know what to say, what words to gray.
Fists in the air, hued as faces – everlasting.

The subdued explanation white as speechlessness,
White in some long faces that are everlasting.

In a distance is the bridge like the City's brow:
Beyond, there won't be faces as everlasting.

Separation offers a darker raspberry
Like the time's spirit in faces – everlasting.

Absence is how we live in each other's silence
In subliminal shouts, faces everlasting.

We're condemned as the eternally out of place.
Protests go on and on, faces everlasting

Independence Day Celebrations

so much
depends

upon William's
suggestion

to put his "red wheel
barrow"

in the middle of
the City square

Jack

Largest humanoid skeleton preserved,
Measuring 14 feet 6 inches, housed in
The *Museum of Cebuano Peculiars* –
Adjudged by international experts/auditors
As "having the second best collection of its kind,"
After the *Believe It or Not* museum in *The Palace*
By the Pasig river. The collectibles
My pet hobby after I accomplished
The biggest Philippine greed per capita empire –
Golden Eggs, Inc. – ubiquity umbrella over
What and where Filipinos and the country's
Visitors eat and drink; how they live, travel,
Get healthier; where to heal or convalesce;
Spend holidays, anniversaries, pastimes;
Grow savings; how to connect communication
Dots; where to educate their children.
This distraction of scouring the island
Of Cebu for brow-raisers a balancing
Respite from climbing life's beanstalks –
Obsessions making every step a challenge
To my will of reaching the top,
Merciless in getting what I want,
Not necessarily what I need.
Conspiring with my professional
Diggers, bribers, buyers, tracker teams
Calms my mind like cups of chamomile tea.

Tomorrow, my 85th birthday, I'll be revealed
As sole benefactor who provokes Cebuanos

Into thinking they're more gigantic than
Self-appraisals, rarer than others think,
Unworldly, X-factored to excel in art, music,
Poetry, in measuring any angle of the universe
And the universal with precision, Alpha Centauri
Not that far from our evolving crafts.
I'll be receiving a plaque made from the same
Axed tree. I've one last surprise to tickle
The world's CEOs and bring the house down
Before retiring as Chairman of everything I see
To be the full time granddaddy of them all:
My harp singing the keynote address.

Aliens vs. Predators

They who don't speak our language
Put their money where our mouths aren't.

They who represent our gullibility
Fill Congress with dogs and trees

They vs. they
Fighting over how laws should protect us
From prosperity.

Pied Piper

This enslavement to my instrument
Follows endless under the table contracts,
Under the carpet anomalies and permits,
Lies for the people's hopes, taxpayer
Pesos pinched, ghost clerks hired,
Men of your political opponent fired,
Substandard structures killer quakes
And waves desire. Music is how
The hideous attains art, my tunes
Like echoes of your unfulfilled promises
To pay. Rats rise from your hidden wealth,
Greed's sewers clogged with leaves
From your family tree. Your name
Stenches the air. I keep returning
To my despair, this yearn to stop
Leading to where justice prevails
But there will always be someone
Like you, so on and on I play this melody,
Till your hypnotized child takes your
Handgun and pumps a bullet in his brain

Momus

Zeus expelled me from Mount Olympus after my
Yakking improvisatory mimicry and onomatopoeic
Expressions of syllabic cooing mooing bang buzz and
Whippoorwill baby sounds made other gods suspect
Variations of my sadistic humor alluding. My cryptic
Ululations, blabbering with animal grunts, mirrored
Tyrannical Zeus' 140-character drivel. He would
Send his audiences head-spinning into confusions,
Ricocheting slurs and non sequiturs like silver bullets,
Quick-tempered King of Heavenly Yes-Beings, parodic
Pet peeve. This lecher rants like he has all the answers,
Ordering sycophants whimsically, contemporary
Nero, onion-skinned sign-of-the-times psychopath,
Mouthing the unprintable, showing off ignorance. I
Love his colorful language – pluperfect for mockeries,
Keen-eyed satires. Power is comedy-prone, politics the
Juiciest jabberwocky. I pleasure in praising with
Insults, throwing blames like bonuses to the corrupt, my
Harlequin heart hula hooping. I delight in poeticizing
Gobbledygook, aping iconoclasts, living among
Filipinos – the stormy planet's most resilient people,
Easily the happiest and the most welcoming. I'm
Delving in the written word's itch for annoying fun,
Caricaturing the rich, speechwriting for the popular
Bipolar bigotry granddaddy, perfecting on page his
Anger's arrhythmia, his full moon glossolalia

Penguin

Anger hanging low like a rotting jackfruit,
Bounty of curses for befuddled audiences.
Craftiness is silver as my walking cane,
Deviltry a day-long lure and I'm helpless.
Entertainer with lavender lipstick, I'm master
Feigner, falconer of pretensions, jack who
Graduated from all tirades to all-out tyranny,
Hippopotamus driven crazy by sounds and
Insects honing the control freak mentality.
Jeopardy, if double, is a doppelganger,
Knavery like a bowtie. I'm smacked with
Loquacity, my heart wearing dancing shoes.
Making it to the not quite female shortlist
Nectarine as night. I'm not divulging the
Oswald Cobblepot teaser, the Gotham
Pulchritude. I need no reasons to cry,
Quarantining my desires en plein air. I
Ruminate more when gazing if the moon
Slice hints of watermelon, my paintbrush
Tamer than starry soliloquies. Gray shades
Understate the glossolalia I alone hear,
Velvet the color I can't escape when
Wishing for a new savior to be nailed.
Xenomania crowds my canvases with
Yellows, nothing more laughable than a
Zoo of caricatures – painted with insults

Supermoon in the Time of Donald Trump

Vision is made
Of bamboo sticks
And origami paper,
Attached to the heart's string

The sign of the times
At perigee glows like a dilating eye,
The kite like a protest poem
In the sky

Covfefe

If you want to wag the dog, covfefe!
If you want people to take their eyes
    off your hands, covfefe!
If you want to distract the FBI, covfefe!
If you want to distract the media, covfefe!
If you want to calm yourself, covfefe!
If you want anger management, covfefe!
If you want to enrich yourself from
    the environment's degradation
    without people noticing, covfefe!
If you are just simply dumb, covfefe!
If you are faker than the news you peddle,
    covfefe!
If you are corrupt as hell, covfefe!

If you want to covfefe the planet, enjoy!
If you want to covfefe NATO, enjoy!
If you want to covfefe yourself,
    don't bring the rest of us
        with you!
Just covfefe yourself!
We don't give a covfefe!

Not Just Listen, but Hear

Your heart is telling you
Billions of people need this planet, too
Countless animal and plant lives
Live on this planet, too

Your brain is telling you
The desire to join an I.Q. contest
Expired 60 years ago

Your pancreas is telling you
Be compassionate

Your kidneys are telling you
You're septuagenarian already,
Be humble

Your liver is telling you, be kind

Your blood pressure is telling you
Be understanding

Your future gout and rheumatoid arthritis
If you still don't have them
Are telling you
It's okay to kneel
Like it's okay to be black

Your arterial plaques are telling you
Don't block the entry of homeless people

People fleeing political persecutions
People who risk their lives
To hold on to dear life
You may drive away people
But you can't change the course
Of your blood – it will burst
Through a blockage
Even if you don't like it

The Ravaging

After Pablo Picasso's Guernica

Skulduggery of shades put me in.
Grays for taste buds, ground grainy
as doves. I smell blood. Mouths
expel hollow air, and I hear.

Palms like blue cornflowers,
luring to be pulled. Charcoal
bodiless arm and leg, but not
deep as indifference, the world

still a bullring. I can't help but
see Donald Trump, his shaped
hair spearing the horse, painful
neigh my scream your scream.

The sun is a slug, a bullet
lodged in the weak spine.
Light lingers for lies, how we
still believe no one else dies.

The Watchers

Not because we're a threat to them.
Only a hundred years for the Wright
brothers' wooden plane to turn into
the F-22 stealth fighter. So if they

preexisted us for millions of years?
Common to know life terminated
at least twice: a giant space rock and
a flood. Our planet holds the living

principle. We've to be zooed in the
Fermi Paradox. Destroyers most of us,
the living vessel the object of concern.
In plain sight the variable they gave

us to exit the simulation's looping
subroutine: love. But most choose
hate and greed, indifference. They're
now preparing to restart the program.

The Drought

Scorched grounds cracking,
The sun a filament without
a bulb, reckless with heat.
Drops from brows vanish

fast as breath on a mirror,
pavements aglow. a distressed
mind reflected. We pine for
the fountain and the flow.

Who sucked the waters of
our sustenance? Our sorrow
has not leveled down, the other
side of the floodgates still.

Mist is the artifice that won't
disperse. We and our children
suffer, while fullness rushes
towards the bank of the river.

Whale

After Whale (oil on canvas)
By Jeanne Fesalbon Jalandoni

        My love for leaping
    Is your blue-shaped wonder
I shoot into air
    Like submarine
        Tomahawk

    I wheel midair
             Somersault
      Spraying geysers
   Of my delight
Fountains of joy

But I must be mindful,
As the seven seas have
More Japanese whalers
Than the senryū of their foibles
No one writes

About the Author

Jonel Abellanosa lives in Cebu City, the Philippines. His poetry has appeared in numerous journals, including Rattle, New Verse News, McNeese Review, Mojave River Review and Star*Line , and been nominated for the Pushcart Prize, Best of the Net and Dwarf Stars award. "Songs from My Mind's Tree," has been published in 2018 by Clare Songbirds Publishing House (New York), which will also publish, "Multiverse," his full-length poetry collection. His speculative poetry collection, "Pan's Saxophone," is forthcoming from Weasel Press. "50 Acrostic Poems" was published by Cyberwit (India) in March, 2019.

Acknowledgements

The author wishes to thank the following publications where the poems first appeared:

New Verse News – "Convergence," "Children of the War," "Warning: Graphic Images, Not Suitable for Children," "Covfefe," "Not Just Listen, but Hear," "The Ravaging," "The Watchers"
Dissident Voice – "Before and After the Dictator"
Rat's Ass Review – "Momus," "Penguin," "Supermoon in the Time of Donald Trump"
Angry Old Man Magazine – "American Cinquain," "The Temptation of Pope Francis"
PEN Peace Mindanao Anthology (University of Santo Tomas Press) – "Mindanao"
Digital Papercut (Wordpool Press) – "Fish Vendor"
Fox Chase Review – "Demolition Job"
Deep Water Literary Review – "Quatrains"
Immix – "Lovers in a Mural"
The Ghazal Page – "Lovers in a Mural" (Republication)
The Chicago Record – "Independence Day Celebrations"
Pedestal Magazine – "Jack"
Mobius: Journal of Social Change – "Aliens vs. Predators"
The Fifty-Two: Journal of Crime Poetry – "Pied Piper"

www.ingramcontent.com/pod-product-compliance
Lightning Source LLC
Chambersburg PA
CBHW030135100526
44591CB00009B/675